Publishing a Book on Amazon:

7 Steps to Publishing Your #1 Book on Amazon Kindle in Minutes!

Patrick X. Gallagher

"Product names, brands, and other trademarks referred to within this book are the property of their respective trademark holders. Unless otherwise specified, no association between the author and any trademark holder is expressed or implied. Use of a term in this book should not be regarded as affecting the validity of any trademark, registered trademark, or service mark."

All rights reserved worldwide
Copyright © 2013 - 2016

Patrick X. Gallagher
As seen on CBS, FOX, NBC & ABC

v1

Table of Contents

Foreword v

Preface vii

Introduction 1

Chapter 1 – What You Need to Do Before You Start
Publishing on Amazon Kindle 9

Chapter 2 – The 7 Steps to Publishing Your Book
on Amazon Kindle 13

Chapter 3 – What's the Best Category for My Book? 27

Chapter 4 – Manage Your KDP Bookshelf Daily! 31

Chapter 5 – The Importance of 5(*****) Star Reviews 33

Bonus Section 39

About the Author 47

Other Books By: Patrick X. Gallagher 49

SOURCES - Further Reading: Books & Videos for
Reference 51

Recommended Websites for Further Review 53

Questions or Comments? 55

Foreword

When you are a published author, people see you in a different way, their first impression towards you will be different.

They trust you more (sub-consciously).

A book helps you to get media and press attention thus helping you expand your personal brand.

10 Benefits of Becoming a Published Author:

1) **Personal Branding**: A book is like an ad for your personal brand - but it doesn't look like an ad. It's like an enhanced resume.

2) **Authority**: When people see you as a published author of a book, you get instant credibility and authority.

3) **It's Content Marketing**: Every digital marketer knows that one of the best ways in digital marketing to attract traffic is content marketing. A book is nothing but content.

4) **No One Throws Away a Book**: When you gift a book to someone who you want to do business with, the book stays with them permanently. It's like re-marketing at no cost!

5) **Speaker Opportunities**: A book can help you get speaking engagements. A book is a solid proof that you are an expert on a subject.

6) **Get Your Dream Job**: If you are an author, it's a clear signal that you know your field. Your chances of getting your dream job goes up dramatically when you are an author.

7) **Get Into Ivy League Universities**: I don't think Ivy League business schools and universities receive a lot of applications with a book! Imagine the possibilities!

8) **Easier Business Transactions**: You can send an autographed copy of your book to someone who you are about to do business with. It breaks the ice and makes the negotiations easier.

9) **Press & Media Coverage**: Reporters are always looking for comments and citations from experts. And who are perceived as experts in today's knowledge economy? Authors!

10) **The Best Investment**: Publishing a good book costs time and money. But it's the best investment you can make for your personal brand and your company. It increases your earning potential and opens the doors to new opportunities.

The above foreword was provided by **Deepak Kanakaraju**. You can read more from his blog here: http://digitaldeepak.com/

Preface

Thank you for buying this book. You now have access to game changer information.

This book will help you succeed in an area of Amazon publishing that no other book will help you succeed in today.

Do you wonder why your excellent content is not being found on Amazon?

Why is it that your book isn't selling as well as you expected?

There are many books on Amazon publishing; even Amazon has a good book on the details of Amazon KDP, but I find it quite boring and hard to read.

You won't find that with this book.

I will show you how to publish your book on Amazon in 7 Steps that take minutes to complete.

This book comes loaded with help, videos, and the revelation of one game changer tool.

You can then learn how other authors have been jumping ahead of your book(s) because they have access to tools that give them an unfair advantage.

If you are not completely satisfied with this book (I am sure you will be), you can always return it within 7 days.

Get my detailed steps to publishing and find direct access to the tools you will use to get started in minutes.

Enjoy!

Introduction

"The worst day of a man's life is when he sits down and begins thinking about how he can get something for nothing." - **Thomas Jefferson**

The difference between success and failure on **Amazon KDP** can largely be determined by your pragmatic ability to continue and learn from the work you put into your book.

What worked yesterday might not work today!

Even after your writing is complete, you will probably feel the urge to write and update your eBook. Amazon Kindle e-book writing and authoring can be addictive! I know it has been for me.

What makes for a good book on Amazon.com? Many successful authors will tell you their own story.

They may even have published a book on the topic.

There is no single attribute that will determine your success as an author on Amazon KDP, or any other publishing platform.

These *digital* authors, such as **Shelley Hitz, Nicholas Black, Tom Corson-Knowles, Von Money, Mark Coker, Ryan Deiss, John Locke, Oli Hille, Michael Thomas, Guy Kawasaki, Jason Matthews, Robert C. Worstell, Kindle Direct Publishing, Lucinda Sue Crosby, Phyllis Zimbler Miller, Scott James, Stephan Little, Blythe Daniel, Jeff Richards, S. J. Scott** and **Steve Scott,** will all have their own story to tell.

My belief is that you have to cover everything after your book is launched before it is actually complete and ready to be published. In other words, 60% of the success of an eBook will be down to how much you spend on planning.

This book will help you do that.

You must have a plan, a well written plan that details the details.

The marketing plan is a very important part of that plan. You must also understand and know about all the **FREE** tools you have at your disposal.

Even the paid tools you can use for launching and maintaining the success of your eBook are something that you should learn and become an expert in.

Of course, you may just prefer to hand these tasks off to someone else. Today in the publishing industry, we outsource and crowd source!

Writing good content, sharing your ideas, and the way you process the tasks are not enough to be successful on Amazon.

The best you can do to ensure your eBook is successful is to learn all the little nuances to Amazon KDP that may prevent your book from selling well.

In my experience, the time best spent is the time you spend on your marketing plan. How will you market your book? Who are your customers? Why will they be your customers?

Why will they buy your book? What is different about your book, as compared to a competing author in your genre? What will be your starting price, etc.?

The most successful authors are those who do not rely solely on their writing and/or typing skills!

These successful authors will have invested and re-invested a boatload of money on learning about marketing and selling their content.

Some authors who self-publish may want to spend their profits on themselves. They may even spend about 3% of their income on learning and promoting their content.

You should do the same.

My own success criterion has been to publish "**secrets**" that will help others to get ahead a lot faster and with more money, remaining in their pocket.

This will be money you can re-invest in your book and YOU. With that being said, you will find at least one secret in this book that will help you save hours of your time.

That alone is worth the price of this book many times over. As someone once said, "Time is money." With this book you will save time and spend it focusing on your book making money!

Cheers to you! Here is to your success in publishing your next book on the Amazon Kindle Platform (KDP).

If you read the kindle version and got as far as here, "**looking inside**" this eBook, and you do not have an Amazon Kindle device, you can get a free Kindle Reader online that works on your personal computer. This will let you read this book and others instantly, goto http://read.amazon.com/about to get it now.

Why I Wrote This book

"To be engrossed by something outside ourselves is a powerful antidote for the rational mind, the mind that so frequently has its head up its own ass." -*Ann Lamott*

Why did I write this book?

A lot of my clients and friends were asking me, how do you publish an eBook on Amazon Kindle? I kept referring them to other Kindle authors.

These were the authors whose *How to Publish on Amazon* eBooks I had read.

Then I thought, I am not going to publish one book myself, I am going to publish several, if not more! I essentially wrote this book for your benefit and mine. To be honest with you, I needed something I could refer to when I needed it for the next eBook. A working handbook, available 24/7.

I believe you need the same help, available anytime.

This book is that handbook you will refer to as often as you need it and whenever you need to publish your next book on **Amazon Kindle Direct Publishing (KDP).**

Now, whenever I have a client, or friend, or family member who wants to publish their next greatest eBook, I can refer them to this book.

I recommend you follow that advice and do the same when you have read and used the book.

If you are an *Amazon Prime Member*, you can even loan this book to your friends and family. Isn't that great? I think it is so cool! The Amazonians have got book selling all figured out.

Now if only they could make the publishing part easier and faster to use! It currently takes between 12 to 24 hours to get your book live after you have uploaded it.

You are going to be using the Amazon KDP tool fairly often. There have been times when I wish I remembered how to do certain things within the Amazon KDP tool.

Like, for example, if you use html as your source for content, how can you easily ensure that the *go to shortcuts will work*?

I spent hours and hours reviewing the Amazon forums, but very few of the comments revealed how you could guarantee stuff would work before you published.

Such as, like I said earlier, ensuring the go to short cut (bookmark hyperlink) works the first time. There are so many eBooks that have this missing!

Would it work on all Amazon platforms, including competing tablets - like the Apple iPad®? I only found out it did not work when the book was already published.

Fixing the issue could take 24 hours and more.

Enter this book. I show you how to do it in **7 Steps** and publish your content in minutes.

From the outset, no application installation is required. As an author, you will need to constantly remind your readers of that fact!

All you need is an Amazon KDP supported browser, liked Firefox or Chrome, and an account setup on Amazon (http://kdp.amazon.com).

When you start to get the hang of the publishing platform you can move straight to the free tools, or others that you can find online.

How much time do you have? If you are like me, you have very little right? Enter this book. It shows you how to do the necessary actions before you need to do them.

A little trick I learned from reading many books: You can create physical items much faster when you, visualize to materialize.

7 Steps to Publishing Your #1 Book on Amazon, will help you get your results more quickly, as you will have carefully reviewed these steps and can refer to them when you are ready to publish.

I lost several days' sales $$$ because I did not know how to do certain things and I missed content validation in my book before I uploaded it to Amazon.

I will share with you how you can quickly validate content without buying a Kindle tablet or reader. I still cannot believe how many Amazon customers and readers believe they need to buy an Amazon Kindle to read Kindle eBooks.

That's simply not true.

You don't even need an Amazon Kindle to read this book. You can use the **Amazon Cloud Reader** (aka a supported web browser), or download the Amazon Kindle Reader app - http://amzn.to/1a1VUtf

In the link above you will gain access to the many e-book readers that Amazon has provided an app. for you. This includes: Smartphones, Mac, Windows 7 & 8, tablet including Android.

Bonus Section

In the bonus section, I will share with you some secrets and tools that other authors are using to get the sales you may not be getting. They are keeping this secret from you. I call this a game changer.

Why can't you have access to this information as well? You can with this e-book!

The Top 10

Aim high from the start. Don't aim to sell one book! Aim to get in to the top **10 of Amazon rankings** almost immediately by managing your book from the moment it is published.

Enrolling your book in KDP Select can be one strategy you can employ that will help you get there.

Now you can also use Amazon's "Promote and Advertise" button in KDP.

Why You Should Read This Book

This book will help you level the playing field and compete with other successful authors who have spent **oodles** of money to get ahead of other authors.

You can do the same by buying this book and using some of the tools I have recommended. They are listed in this book and additional tools are also mentioned at the end of this book.

My goal with this book is to increase the number of Amazon published authors by at least 10%. If you haven't published good content on Amazon, then you simply do not exist!

You should also have access to the tools that some authors are using to get ahead of everyone.

The publishing industry can be a tough industry to crack if you do not know the rules of the game!

What are you waiting for? Start reading this book and get published today! Don't let luck be the deciding factor to your success.

Chapter 1 –
What You Need to Do Before You Start Publishing on Amazon Kindle

"If you don't make mistakes you're not working on hard enough problems. And that's a big mistake." -*Frank Wilczek*

A short list of Items you need:

1) A professionally designed eBook cover. Fiverr.com, or Upwork.com may not get you where you need to be.

2) Your content available in doc, mobi, or html format. There are other formats supported, but those are the best formats you should consider uploading to Amazon KDP.

My own preference is to upload the mobi file, which I typically create from my html content. Why? Well, I prefer that format because I know it will appear correctly when it gets published.

I can also drop in my **pre-prepared OPF file** using the Kindle Previewer App.

3) The title of your book should be ready for prime time. It should be a book title that you have completed key word research on.

4) Kindle Previewer App. You can download it from this link, http://bit.ly/12Hwd03, and you can also download this in the Section 6 on Amazon KDP where it says, "**Preview Your Book.**"

Just click on the instructions and then click on the link that says, "Click here." You can see this in the screenshot below. AmazonKDP has now enhanced the online previewer.

Screenshot o

Enhanced Previewer

Using the enhanced previewer requires a few simple steps:
1. **Download a preview file of your book by clicking the "Download Book Preview File" button**
   If this is your first time using the enhanced previewer, you will need to download the program beginning with Step 2. Otherwise, skip ahead to step 4.
2. **Download the correct previewer by clicking either Windows or Mac**
3. **Install the Kindle Previewer from the downloaded file.**
   If you get a message telling you that the "program may not have installed correctly" click "Cancel".
4. **Open the Kindle Previewer and select "Open Book" from the file menu.**
5. **Find your book, open it and take a look!**
6. **If you would like to make any changes to your book after you preview it, you will need to make those changes to the file you uploaded. Once you have made those changes, you should upload the edited file and preview it again.**
7. **When you are satisfied with the format of the book, come back to this page and click "Save and Continue" to continue the publishing process.**

For more detailed instructions on downloading your preview file and previewer, click here.

5) Your marketing plan. Will you use social media? What will be your starting price point? Will it be high, or will it be low?

6) A good understanding of what it will cost you to publish! Publishing on Amazon may be FREE, but your time has to be considered, as well as any strategy to use the media to announce your book being published

7) A long list of book reviewers. Who will review your eBook as soon as it is published? You can also send them a "Reviewers copy" of the eBook. That way they can write the review as soon as your eBook gets published. The reviewers copy can be a gift sent through your Amazon online account

8) An interview schedule. Will you manage your own PR? Maybe have your own virtual book tour?

9) What sales targets do you want to meet and by when?

10) You need to have read the Amazon Terms and Conditions. You can access it here: http://bit.ly/Amazon_TandC. Also, do read up on DRM*.

You might annoy your potential readers if you do not understand the impact of DRM:
http://en.wikipedia.org/wiki/Digital_rights_management

11) You will need an internet connection too. I uploaded the first version of the eBook version of this book while on holiday in the Bahamas!

Timothy Ferris made his decision based on asking his followers to help him decide if he should enable DRM or not.

Here is a link to him discussing Amazon/E-books on his blog: http://bit.ly/16hwJ9Z

Chapter 2 – The 7 Steps to Publishing Your Book on Amazon Kindle

"People say that what we are seeking is a meaning for life. I don't think this is what we are really seeking. I think what we are seeking is an experience of being alive." *-Joseph Campbell*

Create your KDP account

The first time you go to Amazon Kindle Direct Publishing (KDP), you will need to set up an account with your personal details. You may wish to use your Amazon.com email profile, or use a new one.

You will get this screen shot below.

Screenshot 1

Sign In

What is your e-mail address?
My e-mail address is:

Do you have an Amazon.com password?
- I am a new customer.
  (you'll create a password later)
- I am a returning customer,
  and my password is:

Sign in using our secure server
Forgot your password?
Has your email address changed?

Once you have an account setup, you will be presented with the screen below.

Screenshot 2

Step 1

Click on Bookshelf, if it is not already selected. Then you will see from the above screenshot (screenshot 2) that the Bookshelf menu item is bolded. Click the Amazon orange button,

"Add new title."

What's your book title?

Enter your book title in this step. The book title must match your actual book title. Amazon has a warning that your book will not be published if it is different in any way, such as with extra words inserted for SEO. See **Screenshot 3**.

Screenshot 3

1. Enter Your Book Details

Book name
New Title 1
Please enter the exact title only. Books submitted with extra words in this field will not be published. (Why?)

☐ This book is part of a series (What's this?)

Series title   Volume

Edition number (optional) (What's this?)

Publisher (optional) (What's this?)

Description (What's this?)

4000 characters left

Book contributors: (What's this?)
[Add contributors]

Enter the edition number

Prior to entering the edition number, you may wish to click on the "*this book is part of a series*" button and add extra words here, which will help potential customers find your eBook.

Keep in mind, though, that this will elongate your eBook title, including the sub-title. In the edition number section leave it blank, or enter 2 if it is the second edition, etc.

The first book edition is always automatically set to 1.

Publisher of the book

For publisher, enter your name, or leave it blank. I recommend entering your name as the publisher. You can enter a cool name like: **TCK Publishing USA,** etc.

Book description

In the description section, you will write your 600-700 word description of your book.

You should understand that in this section of step 1, this is one of the most important sub-steps.

See the tips section for more information.

Under the book description there is a button to add additional contributors, such as: Illustrator, Translator, and Editor, etc. Click the add contributors button, as shown in **Screenshot 3**.

You can also fill in the **ISBN number**, language of the book, and the publication date. Unfortunately, you cannot set a pre-scheduled date for the eBook publication on Amazon KDP.

For the ISBN number, keep in mind that a paper back and a digital eBook must have their own unique number. In my opinion you do not need an **e-ISBN** number to publish on Amazon KDP.

Amazon will actually assign your e-book its own unique number, starting with an "A."

Tip 1: Populate the book description with as many words possible. Describe why your book is great and why your readers will want to read it. Essentially this is your "sales copy."

Tip 2: Use your **7 keywords** that you will define and enter in **Step 3**. Again, this is one of the most important parts of publishing on Amazon. You should aim to sprinkle 3-5% of the total word count with your 7 keywords.

Tip 3: You may wish to outsource this part of your eBook self-publishing. The book description can be delegated to an expert in copy-writing. Find a sales copy-writer who can write "*Oceanfront*" book descriptions.

Step 2

Enter your publishing rights. Essentially this is a verification step by Amazon to ensure you own the rights to the content you are publishing. Assuming you click on, "This is not a public domain work...," etc.

Amazon will use their plagiarizing filter to ensure it's not already published content. See Amazon KDP forums for more information.

You will be surprised how often people try to publish other author's content to make a fast buck or two. See **Screenshot 4**.

Screenshot 4

2. Verify Your Publishing Rights

Publishing rights status: (What's this?)
- This is a public domain work.
- This is not a public domain work and I hold the necessary publishing rights.

My assumption is that you will click on the second option button: This is not public domain work and I hold the necessary publishing rights.

Step 3

This is second of the most important steps of the 7 Steps to Publishing Your E-book on Amazon Kindle. I will refer to it again in **Chapter 4**, later on in this book. You can only enter **2 categories** and **7 keywords** in this step.

See my eBook, Amazon Secrets Revealed for my insider tips you can use to improve search rankings on Amazon.com.

Also, in step 3, called: Target Your Book to Customers, you are required to enter the following information. These are: Categories, Age Range (optional), U.S. Grade Range (optional) and Search keywords.

Amazon Book Categories

When you choose your Amazon eBook categories, make sure you have selected 1) the first category that best matches your book genre for non-fiction, or fiction, etc.

Then 2) for the second category, select a category that has very few book sales in it.

In the bonus section I include a link to a cool tool you can use to understand what constitutes few book sales, etc., in terms of author book rankings.

The opportunity to enter your **7 keywords** in **Step 3** will help your customers find your book if they do not use the category section of Amazon.com. It also helps with SEO outside of Amazon.

This **Step 3** should be part of the marketing strategy that you spend most of your time learning to manage and manipulate. Otherwise you will find that your book will sell few copies.

Few people understand the algorithm that Amazon uses to automatically put your book in different categories. For categories different from what you specified in this section, see **Screenshot 5**.

Tip 1: If you can't find a category when choosing categories for your eBook and know that it exists on Amazon.com you can select: **Non-classifiable**.

As you can see in **Screenshot 5,** I have selected this category first. You must scroll to the bottom of the choose categories to see it listed (on the left hand side).

Screenshot 5

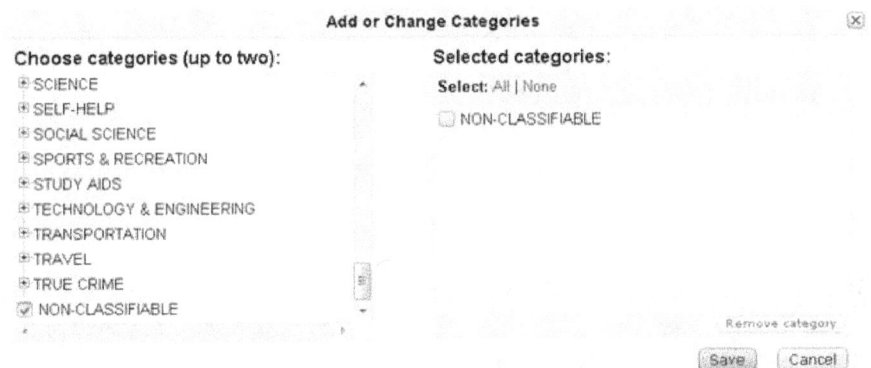

Once you have submitted your eBook to be published, you can then ask **Kindle Support** to move your book into the category you specify in your personal email to them.

For reference, their email address is: **kdp-support@amazon.com**

Step 4

Select Your Book Release Option.

Originally this option was not available on KDP. Now you can offer your customers the pre-release option. This means that customers can pre-order your eBook up to 90 days before you release your eBook.

See screenshot 5.1.

Screenshot 5.1

4. Select Your Book Release Option

Please select if you are ready to release your book immediately or if you would like to make it available for pre-order (What's this?)

○ I am ready to release my book now

● Make my book available for pre-order

   Set a release date for your book

   [   ]

Step 5

Upload or create your book cover.

Referring back to **Chapter 1**, you should already have your cover image created. You absolutely do not want to be publishing a book without a professionally designed book cover.

Remember the old saying, "You get what you pay for in life..," or something like that.

The point is the more you spend on creating the cover image the higher the chance it will be professionally designed and look good.

You can find good eBook cover designers on Upwork, or elance.com. You can find graphic designers on other sites as well, such as on fiverr.com, but I believe you get what you pay for though!

The best quality design specifications indicated by Amazon are: 625 pixels on the shortest side and 1000 pixels on the longest side.

The best quality on high definition devices, the longest side of the cover image should be 2500 pixels.

Go here for further details: http://bit.ly/155qZvc

Step 6

You should upload your book content for this step. I recommend you upload the mobi file you will have created using the Kindle application, **Kindle Previewer**.

Here is a link to the Amazon Kindle Previewer application: http://bit.ly/12Hwdo3

There is also a user guide in pdf and mobi format for you to review.

I use the Kindle Previewer Application to ensure I have a fairly accurate idea of what the eBook content will look like on most Amazon platforms.

Then I do not have to wait for the book to go live to understand what the eBook looks like!

In **Step 6** you either choose Enable DRM, or do not enable digital rights management. Take some time to read up on this controversial topic.

Apparently Tim Ferriss released one of his books to http://www.bittorrent.com and there are other authors who have had their books released to BitTorrent without their consent.

The final part for **Step 6** is to upload your content to Amazon KDP. Locate your .mobi file and browse for your file. Then click Upload book. See **Screenshot 6**.

Note: Amazon KDP currently supports these file formats: doc, html, pdf, and ePub (Mobi).

Screenshot 6

6. Upload Your Book File

Select a digital rights management (DRM) option: (What's this?)
○ Enable digital rights management
◉ Do not enable digital rights management

To enable pre-order for your book, at this time you must submit either the final version of your book file or a draft manuscript. (Why?)
○ This is the final version of my book for release.
◉ This is a draft manuscript and is not ready for release.

Book content file:

[Browse]

Step 7

Choose your pricing and royalty.

How much do you want to sell your eBook for? The default of $2.99 automatically ensures you get the 70% royalty where applicable. See Screenshot 7.

Screenshot 7

9. Set Your Pricing and Royalty

KDP Pricing Support (Beta)
See the relationship between price and past sales and author earnings for KDP books like yours.

View Service

KDP Pricing and Royalty

  Effective January 1, 2015, list prices for EU marketplaces include VAT.
Learn more about VAT

Please select a royalty option for your book. (What's this?)

○ 35% Royalty

● 70% Royalty

The previous choice was verifying your publishing territories, but for the purpose of this book I have listed the most important steps.

As you can see from Screenshot 7, there are several costs associated with publishing a book on Amazon KDP.

If you have the 70% royalty rate, that means you get to pay Amazon 30% of what you make. On top of that are the delivery costs. This is calculated by the size of the file you upload to Amazon KDP.

Keep an eye on your file size. If you have a lot of images in your eBooks like I do, you will lose quite a bit more of your royalty check to Amazon.

If you have large content to send to the millions of connected devices that download your eBook, you will know at the end of the month. Plan ahead and review this delivery cost link below.

Link: http://bit.ly/111t3EC

Step 7

Enable Kindle book lending.

There are actually 2 sub-steps in this step: Step 7. 1) Decide to lend your book. All books are enrolled by default. Step 7.2) Acknowledge the Terms and Conditions and then publish.

Step 7.1

Lending of your book is really a great deal. Even better is that, if you decide to enroll your book in the KDP Select Program, you get a share of the spoils.

Right at the top of Amazon KDP it will show you if your book is already enrolled. You can choose not to enroll you eBook for a further 90 days automatically.

I won't cover all the details, as you can see this information within Amazon KDP. The main points are that you get a share of a $6 million annual fund. As of October 2016, the fund is $12 Million.

The share of the fund is based on how often Kindle customers borrow your book. I like it because it also counts towards your author ranking as an eBook sale.

The downside is that once your book is enrolled in KDP Select, it cannot be offered elsewhere, like on **Nook,** or **Ejunkie,** etc.

Enrolling your book in KDP Select allows you to reach a new audience in the USA and UK (Amazon Prime) and you can also promote your book for FREE. You get 5 FREE Days for every 90 days of enrollment.

Step 7.2

The last part is to accept the Amazon KDP Terms and Conditions. Here is the link to it again:
http://bit.ly/Amazon_TandC

Now sit back and go get a cold one! Come back in 12 hours for English eBooks (up to 72 hours for other languages) and the email account you registered will be sent an email once it has gone live.

Congratulations! Now there is more success for you to accomplish.

Tips

Here are some quick tips to remember when publishing on Amazon KDP.

1) It takes about 12 hours for your book to go live in English language countries.

2) When you add your book description and then edit it in Author Central your book description will no longer be editable on KDP (only Author Central).

3) Edit your 7 keywords as often as you feel necessary perhaps once a month, or every 2 weeks.

4) Experiment with pricing. When your book is selling well, raise the price!

Note: In KDP there are some additional steps, which I have not included in this eBook. These are: Preview Your Book and Verify Your Publishing Territories.

Chapter 3 –
What's the Best Category for My Book?

"Genius is only a superior power of seeing." -*John Ruskin*

Category Confusion

The hardest part about publishing on Amazon KDP, for me, is figuring out in which category my book will sell well.

You have to ask yourself, how will my customers find my book? And so, how do they search for your book?

Do they use the search bar and type in a keyword, or do they navigate the categories listed out on the Amazon.com website?

In any case, you need to have both scenarios covered. For category selection, my strategy is that you put your book in a category that has fewer sales first.

For the second category, you can put your book in the correct genre category, the one that is relevant to your book content.

For example if your book is about Web Marketing, there is a book category for that. Not all content will have a direct relationship with existing Amazon book categories.

Look for books that are similar to yours in content and add it to the category that best suits you and your book. Essentially, you want to be in the top 100, or even better the top 10, as soon as possible.

Be ready each week to move your book around if you do not hit your target numbers.

Example from one of my eBooks:

I wanted to get my book to *number one* using the information I had recorded after months of testing and watching the results.

I put my book in a category that did not have many sales, and within a few days it made #1. Here is the screenshot I recorded earlier.

Here is the result once I had put in place the information I had learned through testing and experimenting with different categories.

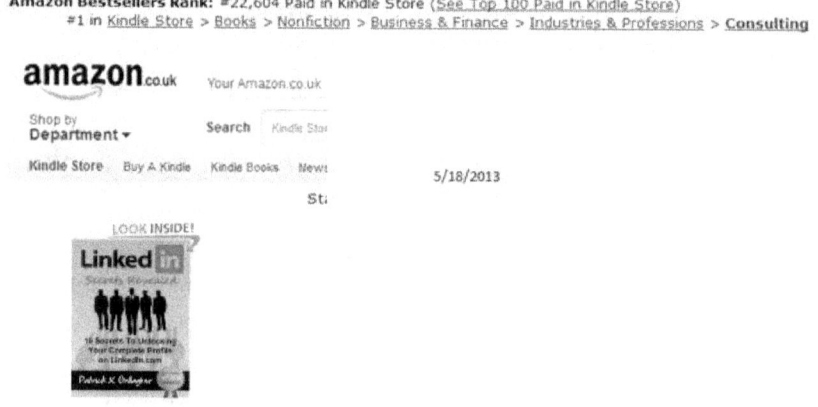

Here is some help from Oli: How to Change your Amazon KDP Kindle Book Categories: http://bit.ly/11RrJAb

In September 2013, I finally cracked the code in getting my eBooks on the best seller list consistently. It takes time, so keep at it and you will succeed as well!

Here is a great example of that code cracking:

Product Details

File Size: 1225 KB
Print Length: 89 pages
Publisher: Patrick X. Gallagher; 1 edition (September 24, 2012)
Sold by: Amazon Digital Services, Inc.
Language: English
ASIN: B009GBTEI8

Oct. 9th, 2013 - #1 in 3 categories

Text-to-Speech: Enabled
X-Ray: Not Enabled
Lending: Enabled
Amazon Best Sellers Rank: #2,091 Paid in Kindle Store (See Top 100 Paid in Kindle Store)
   #1 in Kindle Store > Kindle eBooks > Business & Investing > Careers > Job Hunting > Resumes
   #1 in Books > Business & Investing > Industries & Professions > Consulting
   #1 in Kindle Store > Kindle eBooks > Business & Investing > Industries & Professions > Consulting

Chapter 4 – Manage Your KDP Bookshelf Daily!

"Just set it and forget it!" -*Ron Popeil*

Daily management of your Amazon KDP Bookshelf

You should spend some time each day reviewing your book stats. One time I was glad I made this part of my daily regime!

If not I would have lost more than a day's book sales, due to one book being taken offline. In case you are interested, I got an email from Amazon KDP support that detailed that there were missing image issues. I had that fixed and uploaded the fixes within 24 hours.

Getting on the best seller list should be your primary goal. Once you have cracked the code (using KDP Select on the right days of the week) and chosen the right categories for your book, you will see your book sales take off like a rocket.

Kdp.amazon.com

I strongly urge you to login every day if you can. Then check your book sales. Check that you are making daily sales. If you are not, you need to figure out a plan on how to boost your sales. Record your book sales daily for two weeks.

Obvious choices to help boost sales are to tell your friends and family that you have a book, and then use social media to help you even further.

Kindle Direct Publishing Newsletter

This comes out once a month and gets emailed to the email address you use to publish your book. I suggest you read this monthly, as it contains great information about successful authors, and more.

Chapter 5 –
The Importance of 5(*****) Star Reviews

"There is more to life than just increasing its speed." -*Gandhi*

5 ***** Reviews

Getting reviews should be part of your marketing strategy, if not you are going to be starting on the back foot, even before you hit the submit button on Amazon KDP.

There are really some great examples of Industry Leaders who have gotten almost a hundred reviews the day their book has been published. Take Timothy Ferriss as an excellent example.

Here are the main points you must consider about Amazon Book Reviews:

- Make sure your review process is ethical and follows the Amazon terms and conditions. For example do not pay someone to provide a review (see information below from recent Amazon KDP newsletter).

- Get 5 star reviews from people you work with

- Ask family members: the family members that do not live with you

- Ask friends that you spend time with a lot

- Ask anyone else who you believe would help you by reading & reviewing your book

- Casual Browsing - on the Internet (aka web surfing)

Shill Reviews

Eventually even the best will get a *"Shill Review."* What that means is that someone who has actually not read your e-book will want to destroy your reputation. You need to be ready and decide what approach you want to take. Typical signs of a Shill Review are a) False information - indicated by something that demonstrates the reader has not read the book b)

The Reviewer that left a bad review has not given any other reviews on Amazon products.

I received two in the same month and I do not believe in consequences. My approach was to vote the review down and add a comment to one of those reviews. The final approach is to get more reviews, so the most recent negative reviews eventually end up lower down.

Q & A on Amazon's Customer Review Policies

This information is quoted word-for-word - directly from the **May, 2013 Kindle Direct Publishing Newsletter**. You too will get a monthly newsletter when you join the Amazon KDP website.

Question: Are Authors allowed to review another author's book?

Answer: Yes. We very much welcome Customer reviews from authors.

However, if the author reviewing the book has a personal relationship with the author of the book they are reviewing, or was involved in the book's creation process (i.e. as a co-author, editor, illustrator, etc.), that author is not eligible to write a Customer review for that book.

Question: Can I write a Customer review of my own book?

Answer: No. You are not eligible to review your own book, but there are other ways to communicate with your readers on Amazon, such as Author Central: http://amzn.to/IgIoMb

Question: Can I post a Customer Review on behalf of someone else?

Answer: No. Customer Reviews are meant to provide customers with feedback from fellow shoppers. For this reason, you should use the Editorial Reviews section of your book's detail page to share content that is posted on other sites or from individuals who do not have an Amazon account.

You can update the Editorial Reviews section of your book's detail page through your Author Central: http://amzn.to/IgIoMb

Question: Can I ask my family to write a Customer Review for my book?

Answer: We do not allow individuals who share a household with the author or close friends to write Customer Reviews for that author's book.

Customer Reviews are meant to provide unbiased product feedback from fellow shoppers.

Question: Can I pay for someone to write a Customer Review for my book?

Answer: No. We do not allow any form of compensation for a Customer Review other than a free copy of the book provided upfront.

If you offer a free copy of the book in advance, it must be clear that you welcome all feedback, both positive and negative.

Question: A Customer Review is missing from my book's detail page. What happened?

Answer: Reviews are removed from Amazon for one of three reasons:

1) The review did not meet our posted Customer Review Guidelines.

2) The customer who wrote the review removed it.

3) We discovered that multiple items were linked together on our website incorrectly. Reviews that were posted on those pages were removed when the items were separated on the site.

We can only discuss specific Customer Review removals with the person who originally posted the review.

Getting Customer Reviews for your book can be a key component to your success. Take the time to understand Amazon's customer review guidelines and author tools to assure you are maximizing the opportunity.

You can find the full FAQ on Customer Reviews Guidelines here: http://amzn.to/18MtOpJ

Here is one example of an e-book that I recently read that is **against the terms and conditions of asking and receiving reviews on Amazon.com**. How do I know? I checked with Amazon Kindle Support. You will see Amazon's response below the image.

Appendix F: Opportunities to Connect – and to WIN!

We hope you've enjoyed *How to Write a KILLER*

> Did you find this book helpful? Please share a review on Amazon! You will be entered into a bi-annual drawing to win a $50 Amazon gift card, as well as a monthly drawing to win Mary Elizabeth Bradford's award-winning Job Search Success System!

The above image is from a current best-selling book on Amazon Kindle. It is at the end of the book.

Question: Can you get book reviews by offering an Amazon Gift card in return?

Answer: We don't allow authors or publishers to offer any compensation for Customer Reviews...

On September 24th, 2013 Kindle Direct Publishing <kdp-support@amazon.com> wrote:

Hello Patrick,

We don't allow authors or publishers to offer any compensation for Customer Reviews other than a free copy of the product provided up front. All other forms of compensation, including gift cards to purchase the product or product refunds, could be viewed as a conflict of interest by Amazon customers.

For more information on this policy, please review our Customer Review Guidelines
(http://www.amazon.com/review-guidelines). Failure to comply with

our policies may result in the removal of your Amazon.com publishing privileges.

So there you have it - follow the guide-lines from Amazon and you will never be accused of cheating!

Here is one example of the Kindle Direct Publishing (KDP) newsletter you will get, once you are a published author. Link: http://bit.ly/18MwdRc

Start publishing your first book today. Go here https://kdp.amazon.com/self-publishing/signin

Bonus Section

In this section I reveal what some other authors are using to get ahead of You (possibly) and how you can use these tools to save yourself **hours or more of work**.

There are **2 sections** of **Amazon KDP Book Shelf** that present issues to the author that you must overcome to make a sale. These are: a) What are your keywords and b) What are the Book categories that will help you make a sale?

I will focus only on the keywords part in this **bonus** section for you.

There is a keyword tool out there that helps you get the top searched keywords not just on Google, but also on Amazon too. In **Chapter 3** I discuss the best categories to list your book. However, what you can control immediately is the keywords you specify in the Amazon KDP Bookshelf.

Enter the **Game Changer Keyword Tool**. It's called *FreshKey*: *http://bit.ly/16fdbTG* and it was developed by **Ryan Weiss's** software development team. It's an additional cost, but it is well worth the expense, as it also allows you to run research for your blog, or other social media platforms.

There is no limit to how many times you can run this program. It will always give you up-to-date to the hour information about what customers are searching for on Amazon and Google!

It's currently on limited sale for a special price, but according to **Ryan Weiss**, that won't last long. I would expect the price to go up by 10 times what is currently being offered at right now.

Here is a Video Link to it on **YouTube**. You can click on the image below as well to take you there. Or, simply type the below **bit.ly link** in your web browser.

Video Link: http://bit.ly/10TlwmL

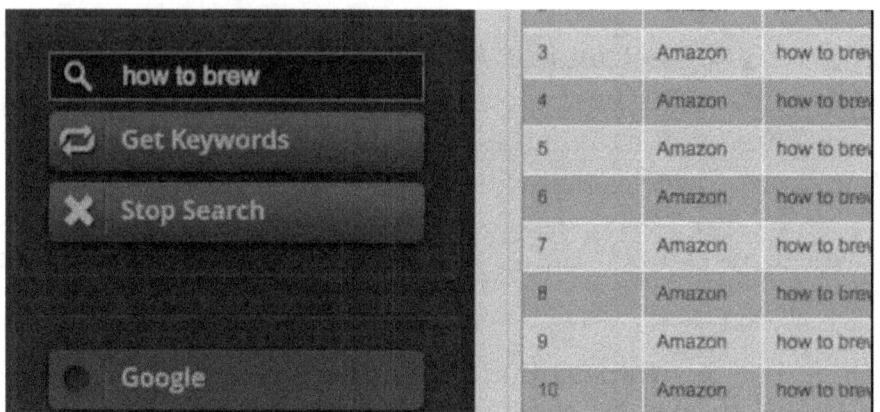

I recommend you to download a copy of it from here today before it gets taken down: http://bit.ly/16fdbTG

Experimenting with Cover Images on Amazon Kindle

This is a really cool application that I discovered. It runs on Apple Macs and PCs. It's an Adobe application and **currently sells for $20**. I highly recommend it.

The software application also has a **30 day money back guarantee!**

Here is a short list of the benefits I have received using it.

1) Save money by being your own designer using the pre-loaded templates

2) You can use your own images as well

3) It supports cover images for Amazon Kindle

4) It is loaded with over 30 templates already pre-installed and available for use

It's the secret software that Top Online Marketers are using for their books fast.

The Image below is from the website:
http://coverloverapp.com

Important Emails with KDP Support

In this section I list some of the most important and time saving emails I received from KDP after I published my first Amazon Kindle e-book.

This will undoubtedly save you time, as it take Amazon typically 24 hours to respond to their Kindle Customer Support enquires.

Question to KDP: Why can I not download a backup copy of my Kindle Book? These instructions do not work for me.

To download your book content file:

1. From the 'Bookshelf,' select the 'Actions' drop-down menu next to the book you wish to modify.
2. Select 'Edit book details' in the menu.
3. Scroll down to the Book Content section and click 'Preview Book.'
4. Click 'Download HTML.'
5. Choose a location on your hard drive to which to save the ZIP file, then click 'Save.'

Link: To download your book content file:
https://kdp.amazon.com/self-publishing/help?topicId=A1KIW2CNWB4717

Answer from KDP: I checked your account and see that you've uploaded original file in AZW format. For this reason, the "download your book content file" option is not available.

Please upload your original in DOC or HTML. HTML is the best supported format for publishing on KDP, as the desired formatting effects can be easily achieved using the HTML tags.

Learn more on formatting your Kindle content in our Kindle Publishing Guidelines here:

http://s3.amazonaws.com/kindlegen/AmazonKindlePublishingGuidelines.pdf

Question to KDP: I would like an updated copy of the Author's book: LinkedIn Secrets Revealed. ASIN: B009GBTEI8 - link:
http://www.amazon.com/dp/B009GBTEI8

Answer from KDP: Hello,

I understand you would like to get an updated version of "LinkedIn Secrets Revealed..." book on your Kindle. I'll surely assist you.

I've sent the updated version of "LinkedIn Secrets Revealed: 10 Secrets To Unlocking Your Complete Profile on LinkedIn.com (Includes: LinkedIn Books, LinkedIn Success, LinkedIn Kindle, ... LinkedIn Influence, LinkedIn Careers)" to your Kindle

To complete your download, verify that your device is sufficiently charged and your wireless connection is enabled.

To manually activate the download, select Sync & Check for Items from the Home screen menu. Alternatively, you can delete the copy of the book from your Kindle Home Screen and redownload it from [Archived Items / Cloud].

The previous version of your book will be automatically replaced by the updated version.

I hope this helps. Thanks for using Kindle.

Best regards,

Rupam T

Question to KDP: Hi KDP, do authors need to accumulate a certain $$$ amount before getting paid royalties in addition to the 60 day wait time?

Answer from KDP: Yes, there is a minimum threshold which needs to be reached in order for royalties to be paid out.

Royalties accrue on your account until the total amount due is at least $10/$10 CAD/£10/€10/Rs 500/¥1000 if by EFT or $100/$100 CAD/£100/€100 if by check. The EFT threshold for Amazon.com.br royalties is R$20 for Brazilian publishers and R$100 for non-Brazilian publishers.

You can find more information by reading our Terms and Conditions here:

http://kdp.amazon.com/self-publishing/help?topicId=200627430

Question to KDP: Hi KDP, I would like to change Book categories please

Answer from KDP: We prefer publishers make changes to their own book...

Hello,

We prefer publishers make changes to their own book categories to ensure they have full control and are able to make additional changes in the future.

You can ensure your book is added to "Kindle Store > Kindle eBooks > Business & Investing > Small Business & Entrepreneurship > Mail Order" in the Kindle Store by assigning the following path in your KDP Bookshelf:

BUSINESS & ECONOMICS / Mail Order

These choices don't match the website exactly because the options displayed in your Bookshelf are **BISAC categories** (Book Industry Standards and Communications), and the names shown on the Amazon website are **Browse categories**.

To change your book categories:

1. Log into your KDP account at https://kdp.amazon.com

2. Check the box to the left of the book, click "Actions" at the top left, and "Edit book details."

3. Scroll down to "Target Your Book to Customers" and click "Add/Remove categories."

4. Select relevant categories on the right side of the screen and confirm your choice to add or remove.

5. Click on "Save."

6. Scroll down the page and click "Save and continue," which will take you to the "Rights & Pricing" section.

7. Check the box at the bottom of the screen to accept the Terms & Conditions, then click "Save and publish."

About the Author

Patrick Gallagher provides his talent & services to a major Fortune 500 company.

Everything that is shared with you in this book is aimed to help you spend more quality time with your friends and family.

When Patrick is not at work he enjoys spending time reading and learning from other smart people.

Patrick is active in community affairs and regularly volunteers for local charities in the USA. He is originally from the United Kingdom and is married with children.

He currently resides in Sunny, Texas. Where there are only two seasons: Warm season and hot season!

Click on his LinkedIn Profile.

You can also connect with him on his Twitter page. Short Link: http://bit.ly/Odcjqa

One click connect on LinkedIn - http://linkd.in/JLkJUW

Other Books By: Patrick X. Gallagher

LinkedIn Secrets Revealed: 10 Secrets To Unlocking Your Complete Profile on LinkedIn.com
http://bitly.com/12pyCNu

Pimp Your Profile: How to Amplify your LinkedIn Profile on your Mobile Device
http://amzn.to/1Q32mbM

Email Inbox Management: How to Master Your Inbox with Etiquette
http://amzn.to/1OvBOhI

Amazon Secrets Revealed: How To Sell More Books on Amazon.com
http://amzn.to/1lOLLxn

Love or Hate Email...21 Rules to Change Your - I Must Check my Email Habit. Get Back to Work and Make Money Again!
http://bit.ly/Love_Email

Build Your Own Living Revocable Trust: A Pocket Guide to Creating a Living Revocable Trust
http://amzn.to/1CoNUmn

Spirituality in the Workplace: A Study Guide for Business Leaders
http://amzn.to/1CoNUmn

Trapped in a Meritocracy: Cracking the Meritocracy Code: Get Paid More for Valued Performance
http://amzn.to/1zbufrW

Write You Book Outline: How to Create Your Book Outline in 30 Minutes
http://mybook.to/outline

SOURCES -
Further Reading: Books & Videos for Reference

Some of these sources are books that I have read and some are websites that I recommend reviewing for further information. I have included links to my online Amazon Book Library

"How to Change your Amazon KDP Kindle Book Categories,"- http://bit.ly/11RrJAb, by Oli Hille

"How to Change Your Book Cover on Amazon Kindle KDP," - http://bit.ly/11b3dLA, by Oli Hille

"How to Write an Effective Book Description," - http://bit.ly/15d0Coi

"Self Service Cover Design," - http://bit.ly/1ambz9P

"Publish on Amazon Kindle with Kindle Direct Publishing" - http://amzn.to/11o7C1g by KDP

"Building Your Book for Kindle"- http://amzn.to/191JVAZ by KDP

Recommended Websites for Further Review

Web: **Amazon Kindle Direct Publishing** -
https://kdp.amazon.com/self-publishing/signin

Web: **Amazon Kindle Select** -
https://kdp.amazon.com/self-publishing/KDPSelect

Web: **Amazon Kindle Dashboard** -
https://kdp.amazon.com/self-publishing/dashboard

Web: **Amazon Kindle Community** -
https://kdp.amazon.com/community/index.jspa

Web: **Amazon Kindle Help** –
https://kdp.amazon.com/self-publishing/help

Questions or Comments?

Congratulations for getting this far and reading this book! Now that you have read the book and put it to good use, I would love to hear from you.

Connect with me via **View my profile on LinkedIn**.

One last thing, if you believe this book has helped you and is worth sharing with other potential Amazon Kindle readers; please leave a review by **clicking on the button** below. Your review feedback will make the next version even better for future readers.

http://amzn.to/19AB5XJ

On Amazon, all 5 star reviews are like gold! I would really appreciate you leaving a 5 star review - it should take only a few seconds of your time.

For readers outside the US, please also click the *follow* button on the Amazon author page. Go here: http://author.to/LinkedInAuthor

This includes the UK, Canada, France, Australia and Germany etc.

Remember - when you leave a 5 star review I feel like you have given me a gold bar like below!!

Thank You!

Don't forget to leave a review on Amazon.com for others to read and benefit from your feedback!